Girl! What you gonna DO with your MONEY?

Money Matters For Teens

MAX Publishing, LLC

Ti'Juana Gholson

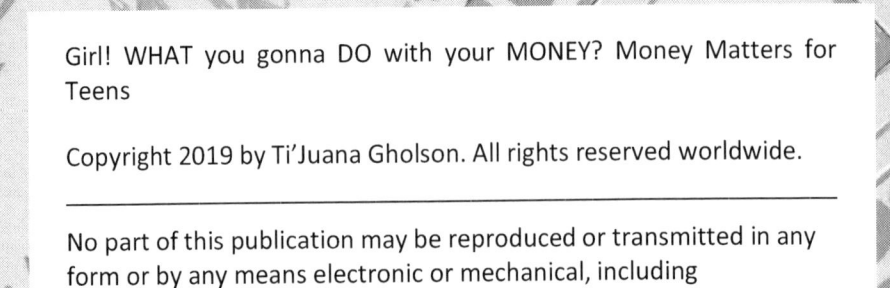

Girl! WHAT you gonna DO with your MONEY? Money Matters for Teens

Copyright 2019 by Ti'Juana Gholson. All rights reserved worldwide.

No part of this publication may be reproduced or transmitted in any form or by any means electronic or mechanical, including photocopying, recording or by any information storage and retrieval system without written permission from the author.

Published in the United States of America

ISBN – 13: 978-1-970097-06-1

Disclaimer/Warning:

This book is intended for lecture and educational purposes only.

This book provides no guarantees of effectiveness for ALL persons. This book is the opinion of the writer and serves as a guide to support lecture or training offered by the writer and team.

Book cover (front and back) and some body illustrations by:
Trevor Lucas – Anamoly Studios, LLC

Editor: Alesha Brown – Alesha Brown, LLC

Published by:

MAX Publishing, LLC

Girl, WHAT you gonna DO with your MONEY?
Money Matters for Teens

Just because you're a TEEN doesn't mean YOU can't DREAM!!!

-TAG

Girl, WHAT you gonna DO with your MONEY?
Money Matters for Teens

Girl, WHAT you gonna DO with your MONEY?
Money Matters for Teens

Dedication

I dedicate this book to my favorite daughter, Ti'Mari Lawren-Antjuanette (inside joke). Baby Girl, *you* have had an up-close look at how money matters to *me*. I hope the example helps you with your financial life journey.

To my future grand-daughters, my sons, my grandsons, my mother Valerie, my granny Mary, my mother-in-love Glenda and my sisters (especially my baby sister Jennifer Marie who allows me to fuss at her about money matters every day). I hope this book encourages you on your everyday financial journey.

To my nieces, goddaughters, cousins, my Sistahood Divas, LLC, my clients and mentees: I want you to know that YOU can do this! If I can, so can YOU!

To my husband Lawrence II and grandsons (Lawrence III and Ro'Mir) who read this book first and put their stamp of approval on it: **THANK YOU** for supporting me!

To my baby grandson Mr. Kase: you'll be reading this and other books before you know it!

I Love you ALL, Always!

Girl, WHAT you gonna DO with your MONEY?
Money Matters for Teens

Girl, WHAT you gonna DO with your MONEY?
Money Matters for Teens

Testimonials

I absolutely love this book and will definitely be purchasing at least four for my older girls! I LOVE how everything is broken down. I love that you break it down so that a teen can understand it but not to where they feel like your speaking to a child. I also love that you told them to ask an adult they trust because sometimes teens aren't comfortable speaking to their parents, especially mine – lol.

Krystal Parker, Lead Teacher
First Baptist Preschool, Newport News, Virginia

Thank you for allowing me to preview [this book] and give feedback. WOW! This is very good! This is good, practical information. I especially like that you asked the young ladies to define words at the end of the chapters. Writing definitions helps to retain words and meanings better, as well as helps to learn how to spell the words.

This book is an awesome research tool for my daughter Rachel, as she is on her financial path already. It's going to help her line things up even better. This book will, hopefully, launch several young ladies into entrepreneurship more smoothly and quicker than they could have ever imagined.

Mary Singleton, Home School Instructor and Entrepreneur
Owner of Mscreations, LLC and Virtually Yours in Hampton, Virginia

This book educates on what teens need to know while they are maturing and turning into working adults. From the beginning of the book, the author discusses acknowledging HOW a person feels about money, paying attention to what a person buys (going out to eat, buying shoes, etc.) and having discipline by learning the difference between needs and wants.

Girl, WHAT you gonna DO with your MONEY?
Money Matters for Teens

This author has hit the hot spots about money head on! As we all know, youth are growing and becoming more independent at an early age and what was learned in college in my day is now being taught in middle and high school. Financial education is a must and I am glad that THIS author thought enough about our youth to take the time to write about it. This book is amazing! It's very well written and would be an asset to high school students as they are required to take a personal finance class. This book is full of knowledge and inspiration to help teens grow and learn about their financial future and "securing the bag"!

Thank you for helping our teens as they become successful adults!

Tawan Silver-Maner, Middle School Guidance Counselor
Newport News, Virginia

Girl, WHAT you gonna DO with your MONEY?
Money Matters for Teens

This Book's Purpose

This book is intended for **YOU**, the **TEEN**, to have a general guide to money matters. This book is designed to go alongside the adult version of the book and to stimulate a conversation between you and an adult you trust.

May this book be the start of your financial education and stimulate questions as well as a desire to learn more about money matters. It's never too early to know why money matters and why it should matter to **YOU**.

So GO Girl and Learn!

With Love,

Ti'Juana A. Gholson, MA

Girl, WHAT you gonna DO with your MONEY?
Money Matters for Teens

Girl, WHAT you gonna DO with your MONEY?
Money Matters for Teens

Foreword

On a cold, dreary day, my 11-year-old daughter comes and advises she is in need of new reading material. After all, we have been in the house for the past eighteen hours and her electronics utilization is limited. *Yes, even in the age of information overload and Google, I make my child pick up an actual book!*

I was very stoked about the secret gem I was about to share with her. This would not be a simple read, however, but something that would educate her, stimulate her mind, engage her as well as bless her. This would be a TOOL, one that would keep on giving for the rest of her life.

There is a need for this dialogue in the younger generation today. Unfortunately, our children and many adults, aren't aware of how to deal with their personal finances or even where to begin. This nugget is an awesome ally.

The author took special time to advise the audience of basic finance words as well as wealth words. She also ensures that they grasp concepts without overkill by being direct. This book will allow your young reader to look back and see memories as they grow and learn. She truly captivates the audience with the truth, yet necessary verbiage on the pages given.

As an educator and former bank executive, I can attest that there is an imperative demand in our homes and schools for this type of knowledge. This book should definitely be a staple in the curriculums across our nation.

Girl, WHAT you gonna DO with your MONEY?
Money Matters for Teens

I am an avid reader and found this to be an easy and comparable read for all ages. You are never too young to learn. The best books present themselves precisely and this one did just that!

I am honored to share this new jewel with my daughter for many reasons, of course, the aforementioned one. I'm also excited because the author is who my child has affectionately referred to as "Auntie Ti" all of her life.

Ti'Juana is a dynamic businesswoman who wears many hats and has now added author to that list. She is most certainly a force to come up against! WORK is her MIDDLE name! This woman has been a wonderful sister to me for the past 11 years and I could not be prouder of her.

~Mrs. La'Quan Driver, MS - High School Teacher
Hampton, Virginia

Girl, WHAT you gonna DO with your MONEY?
Money Matters for Teens

Table of Contents

WHY MONEY *REALLY* MATTERS FOR YOU?	15
HOW DO I FEEL ABOUT MONEY?	19
Common Excuses/Barriers Blocking Wealth	21
Money Blockers	25
Two Words that UNBLOCK money	26
Key Words for Money Matters	28
MONEY DISCIPLINE: HOW TO SAVE	31
Key Words for Saving	35
GETTING IT TOGETHER: CREDIT	39
Key Words for Buying Power	42
FINANCIAL FREEDOM	47
Key Words for Financial Freedom	51
FAILURES	55
SEE – BELIEVE – DO	61
EDUCATE YOURSELF! YES, YOU CAN!	65
Financial Education Homework	66
WHAT DO I DO NOW?	69
ABOUT THE AUTHOR	72
FINANCE JOURNAL	75

Girl, WHAT you gonna DO with your MONEY?
Money Matters for Teens

Girl, WHAT you gonna DO with your MONEY?
Money Matters for Teens

WHY MONEY *REALLY* MATTERS FOR YOU?

Women and men accumulate wealth differently: Women have an unfair disadvantage from BIRTH!

> By simply being born a woman, women have an unfair disadvantage when it comes to wealth accumulation.

YOU, as a young and growing woman, have been historically seen as the "homemaker". This label automatically causes women to not be taken as seriously as men in the workplace.

According to the US Census Bureau and the Labor Department, in 2016 women earned somewhere between 80 cents for each dollar a man earned.[1] Due to lower wages, females are automatically behind the wealth curve.

Do you think that's fair? Well, I believe you can do something about that. *I believe YOU can change that statistic!*

Girl! WHAT your gonna DO with your MONEY?

---

[1] Donnelly, G. (2017 September 13). The Gender Pay Gap Narrowed in 2016. But Only by 2 Cents. Retrieved 13 September 2018, from http://fortune.com/2017/09/13/gender-pay-gap-2016/.

Girl, WHAT you gonna DO with your MONEY?
Money Matters for Teens

A REAL LIFE EXAMPLE:

I know a teen girl named Mary who dreamed of one day becoming very successful and making a lot of money. Mary got a job and worked hard, even as a teenager. She began to make wise decisions to save her money.

Mary started saving for little things like her school clothes and then graduated to saving for bigger things like purchasing a car. Yes, as a TEENAGER, Mary purchased her own car!

Mary learned the value of saving money and seemed to understand early on that if she saved now and made purchases later, she could get the things she wanted and needed without having to owe anybody.

Mary also saved enough money for emergencies. Being a car owner, she had to plan for things like insurance, maintenance (new tires and oil changes) and other unexpected repairs. When emergencies arose, Mary had the money she needed to cover the expenses because she preplanned and saved her money.

Mary grew up to be an amazing businesswoman and she now has more than enough money to cover anything she needs and WANTS to buy. You too can be like Mary and make wise decisions with *your money*.

Did you know you should save some of your money for emergencies?

1

How do "I" feel about MONEY

Girl, WHAT you gonna DO with your MONEY?
Money Matters for Teens

Girl, WHAT you gonna DO with your MONEY?
Money Matters for Teens

HOW DO I FEEL ABOUT MONEY?

Cash, dinero, duckies, cheddar, paper, money, money, money, money... MONEY! EVERYBODY wants it!

"Money is not EVERYTHING," they say. Sure, *money isn't EVERYTHING* until you don't have any.

"Money pays the bills," Mom says.

"Money doesn't grow on trees," Dad says.

Right now all YOU need money for is school lunch, downloading music, filling up the car with gas, getting that new pair of shoes or buying a new outfit at the mall. You may even wonder WHY money is so important. WHY does the world always talk about it? WHY do your parents fight about it?

Why? Why? WHY?

I'll tell you WHY. Money makes the world go around! I want you to shut out everybody else's ideas about money and take time to think about the following questions.

Write your responses in the space provided.

Girl, WHAT you gonna DO with your MONEY?
Money Matters for Teens

✍ How do I feel about Money? ✍

1. How do "I" feel about money?

   _____
   _____
   _____

2. What am I being taught about money?

   _____
   _____
   _____

3. What's being said to me?

   _____
   _____
   _____

4. What's being said around me?

   _____
   _____
   _____

Girl, WHAT you gonna DO with your MONEY?
Money Matters for Teens

Common Excuses/Barriers Blocking Wealth

In your life, do any of the following sound familiar?

- ➢ I don't make enough money.
- ➢ I didn't get paid today.
- ➢ I don't keep money long.
- ➢ I like to shop.

I own a business and I hire people to work for me. Over the years I have noticed that:

> Regardless of HOW much money a person makes, if they don't know how to manage it, they will STILL end up BROKE!

People use money the way they want to use it. Most of the time, without thinking, people spend their money as quickly as they

Girl, WHAT you gonna DO with your MONEY?
Money Matters for Teens

get it. Many people have said to me, "I don't have enough money to save" and I can visibly see why.

I often see people wearing the money they should have saved. These are the people who, even if they can't afford to, they wear designer shoes, belts, fancy nails and designer labeled jeans.

You know these people too. Many of these same people spend money going out to eat *every* weekend, hanging out or doing what my kids call "flossing". You are probably thinking of a few of them now, right?

Well, when you add up those items, you can find an excess of $50 to $100 per month in the average person's budget. Can you believe that? Just by looking at what a person wears, you can see the extra money they have to save?

Of course, there are always exceptions to every rule because EVERYBODY doesn't shop for expensive items or go out and waste money. However, what is not the exception is the fact that most people spend money on *something* they could *live* without. The point is unless you are dirt poor or have NO money coming in, you can FIND EXCESS MONEY *if* you try.

I want you to start thinking about how *you* feel about money. Identifying your feelings now may help you make good money decisions in the future. I want you to try to eliminate early, any barriers that may possibly block your future wealth. It's never too early to start thinking about these things and to start planning for your financial future.

Let's discuss this further during the next exercise.

Girl, WHAT you gonna DO with your MONEY?
Money Matters for Teens

Let's TALK about Money!

✍ **List 5 things you've learned about money** ✍

1._____

_____

2._____

_____

3._____

_____

4._____

_____

5._____

_____

Now discuss these ideas with an adult. Record the results:

_____

_____

_____

Girl, WHAT you gonna DO with your MONEY?
Money Matters for Teens

✍ List 3 ideas YOU have about money: ✍

1._____

   _____

2._____

   _____

3._____

   _____

Now discuss these ideas with an adult. Record the results:

_____

_____

_____

_____

Girl, WHAT you gonna DO with your MONEY?
Money Matters for Teens

Money Blockers

In life, some people have *misfortunes*. These misfortunes can be what I call *money blockers*. Money blockers can come in many forms such as losing a job, getting divorced, overspending or simply not paying attention to where your money goes. These are just a few money blockers but the list can be endless.

In my experience, I have noticed that one of the primary reasons the average person doesn't save enough money is because he/she does not appropriate their money correctly. As stated previously, people spend their money how they *want to* spend it and what they *want to* spend it on. When people do not pay attention to their spending habits, it makes it difficult for them to maintain a good savings plan.

Remember, in order to have money, it is important to carefully appropriate it (devote to a special purpose).

KEY MONEY BLOCKERS:

appropriation

Appropriation

APPROPRIATION!

Girl, WHAT you gonna DO with your MONEY?
Money Matters for Teens

Two Words that UNBLOCK money

Delayed Gratification

What do you mean I have to wait?

But I want what I want and I want it NOW!

Delayed Gratification means to save now and buy later.

Most people don't want to do that because we live in a society of *right now*.

Credit makes it so easy for us to buy stuff now and pay later. This causes us to get into what is called *debt*. BUT, in order to save, you must learn how to wait.

It doesn't take much! If you are **dedicated** and **willing to try**, you can do anything! But the question is, will you delay your wants for your future? Let's discuss ideas for saving in the next chapter.

Will YOU delay your wants for your future?

Girl, WHAT you gonna DO with your MONEY?
Money Matters for Teens

✍ **What things are your *must-haves*?** ✍

_____   _____

_____   _____

_____   _____

✍ **What do you feel when YOU hear "delayed gratification"?** ✍

_____

_____

_____

_____

_____

_____

_____

_____

_____

_____

Girl, WHAT you gonna DO with your MONEY?

Money Matters for Teens

Key Words for Money Matters

Here are a few vocabulary words I want you to research and discuss with an adult.

Write the definitions below:

Delayed Gratification _____

_____

_____

_____

Debt _____

_____

_____

_____

Credit _____

_____

_____

_____

2

Money Discipline How to SAVE

Girl, WHAT you gonna DO with your MONEY?
Money Matters for Teens

Girl, WHAT you gonna DO with your MONEY?
Money Matters for Teens

MONEY DISCIPLINE: HOW TO SAVE

"We don't have enough."

"What do you need money for now?"

"You think money grows on trees?"

Are any of these familiar phrases to you? Maybe you've heard them from a parent or other loved one when you've asked for money.

Why do you think money is always a concern? How do we save so that when we need money it's there? Well, it's actually quite simple.

Money coming in, (any money you receive), is called **INCOME**. Money going out, (any money you owe), is called **EXPENSES**. So in order to save money, your *income* must be greater than your *expenses*.

But FIRST, pay yourself! Set aside an amount of money you want to have to do other things.

1. **Save for emergencies.** You know, like Mary did to make sure she could pay for maintaining her car? And...

2. **Save for fun.** Saving for those extra things you want to do like going to the movies with friends or buying a pair of shoes you've always wanted will keep you from not having money when you *really* need it.

Saving will help you to be able to pay your living expenses *and* enjoy your income. Saving keeps you from totally being without money!

Girl, WHAT you gonna DO with your MONEY?
Money Matters for Teens

What's the key?

Keep your *expenses* (what you owe) at a level where it doesn't take all of your *income* (money you have coming in)!

✍ List 3 ways YOU can save: ✍

1._____

_____

2._____

_____

3._____

_____

A simple savings plan can look like this:

✓	Paying yourself first
✓	Saving for emergencies
✓	Saving for investments
✓	Saving for charity
✓	And then paying your debts

Girl, WHAT you gonna DO with your MONEY?
Money Matters for Teens

NOTE: paying yourself first can help you have money saved for emergencies or for those extras you desire. Paying yourself first can also help you save for later life expenses like retirement. **YOU** decide what you wish to designate that money for.

Income - Expenses = SAVINGS!

Girl, WHAT you gonna DO with your MONEY?
Money Matters for Teens

Girl, WHAT you gonna DO with your MONEY?
Money Matters for Teens

Key Words for Saving

Here are a few vocabulary words I want you to research and discuss with an adult.

Write the definitions below:

Savings _____
_____
_____

Income _____
_____
_____
_____

Expenses _____
_____
_____
_____

Budget _____
_____
_____
_____

Girl, WHAT you gonna DO with your MONEY?
Money Matters for Teens

Key Words for Saving (continued)

Investments _____

_____

_____

_____

Charity _____

_____

_____

_____

Loan _____

_____

_____

_____

Retirement _____

_____

_____

_____

3

Getting it together!
CREDIT

Girl, WHAT you gonna DO with your MONEY?
Money Matters for Teens

Girl, WHAT you gonna DO with your MONEY?
Money Matters for Teens

GETTING IT TOGETHER: CREDIT

Credit: What is it? Have you ever heard about it? Do your parents talk about it?

So what is *credit* and why does it matter? What is credit's relationship with money? Some would say that your *credit* is your report card: it tells how well you pay your bills.

Example: you get a car loan for a shiny new red Mustang. Each month you owe the bank $300 in the form of a loan (or some call it a note).

You owe this money to the bank by the 1st day of each month. When you pay the bank on time, the bank sends a good report to the credit bureaus. If you don't pay the bank on time, they also send a report to the credit bureaus. But this time not so good. Now do you see why I said your *credit* is a report card?

Do you know what a credit bureau is? Go ahead and look it up. Go ahead... do it NOW! And while you're looking up information on what a credit bureau is, answer the following question:

📖 List 3 credit bureaus: 📖

1._____

2._____

3._____

Girl, WHAT you gonna DO with your MONEY?
Money Matters for Teens

There are 3 major credit bureaus. Each credit bureau gives you a score called a ... you guessed it: a **CREDIT SCORE (also known as a FICO score)**. A good credit score is somewhere between 700 and 850.

WHY is this important?

It's important because the better your credit score, the more buying power you have especially for major purchases like a home. Most people apply for a loan known as a mortgage when they want to buy a home. You may also want to start a business one day. Many people apply for a business loan to help them jumpstart their business.

Your credit score helps you get the credit amount (or loan) you want. Credit acts as money: it allows you to borrow money from a bank or other lending institution and gives you time to pay it back. You pay this money back in increments.

Why is this important?

You may not think about it now, but one day you will be an adult and you're going to want to buy a car, a house and maybe even start a business. You may also want to open a checking or savings account. Your GOOD credit score will help you!

Now it's time for some research!

Girl, WHAT you gonna DO with your MONEY?
Money Matters for Teens

Discuss with an adult why you need a good credit score. Record the results:

_____

_____

_____

_____

_____

_____

_____

_____

_____

_____

_____

_____

_____

_____

_____

Girl, WHAT you gonna DO with your MONEY?
Money Matters for Teens

Key Words for Buying Power

Here are a few vocabulary words I want you to research and discuss with an adult.

Write the definitions below:

Credit Score _____
_____
_____
_____

Mortgage _____
_____
_____
_____

Business Loan _____
_____
_____
_____

Bank Account (checking) _____
_____
_____
_____

Bank Account (savings) _____
_____
_____
_____

Girl, WHAT you gonna DO with your MONEY?
Money Matters for Teens

✍ **What financial words were you already familiar with?** ✍

_____   _____

_____   _____

_____   _____

_____   _____

_____   _____

_____   _____

✍ **What new words have you learned from reading this book?** ✍

_____   _____

_____   _____

_____   _____

_____   _____

_____   _____

_____   _____

_____   _____

Girl, WHAT you gonna DO with your MONEY?
Money Matters for Teens

4
Financial Freedom

Girl, WHAT you gonna DO with your MONEY?
Money Matters for Teens

Girl, WHAT you gonna DO with your MONEY?
Money Matters for Teens

FINANCIAL FREEDOM

Remember when we talked about money coming in (income) and money going out (expenses)?

Well, let me add, if you have more money coming in than going out, you *may* consider yourself wealthy. Most people strive to have more money coming in than going out. But I can honestly tell you this is NOT the average person's situation! Why? As we've already discussed, most people do not appropriate their money and save. Most people want what they want NOW therefore not practicing **delayed gratification**.

But what if a person DOES have more coming in than what they have going out? What is THAT called? Additionally, what does it mean when the money coming in is what a person has invested and they no longer have to physically show up to work to receive that money?

Those are great questions and I'm glad you asked! That is also a place that many strive to be. I call it being Financially Free! When a person has more money coming in than going out *AND* they do not always have to show up to work to get it, they are experiencing **FINANCIAL FREEDOM**!

If that's your situation, you too are Financially Free!

Can YOU be financially free as a teen?

Yes, if YOU want to be!

But HOW?

Girl, WHAT you gonna DO with your MONEY?
Money Matters for Teens

Here are a few ways that you can work to become Financially Free:

1. **START A BUSINESS.** You have ideas, right? Well, start a **BUSINESS!**

2. **BUSINESS PARTNERSHIPS.** You have friends with ideas, right? Well, form a **BUSINESS PARTNERSHIP!**

3. **REAL ESTATE INVESTOR.** Thinking about buying a home one day? Well, buy additional homes to become a **REAL ESTATE INVESTOR** (a Landlord). *This is where having good credit may be important.*

4. **INTELLECTUAL PROPERTY.** You are pretty smart, right? And you can create things? Well, if you do, write a book about it, get patents made and one day you will receive what they call **royalties** or money for things that *you* created! Sounds cool right? Do your research and tell me what **INTELLECTUAL PROPERTIES** (aka IP) are. I'm waiting to hear your response:

    (www.tijuanagholson.com)

5. **COMMODITIES.** Remember earlier we talked about having money for bills and things like gas and oil? Well, anything that people spend money on, others *make* money on. This is what being an **investor** is. YOU can invest in everyday things that people have to spend money on. These everyday things are called **COMMODITIES** (like gas and oil). Google it and find out more.

6. **E-COMMERCE.** Many people your age are becoming famous on the internet for selling products, making music, doing comedy, etc. All of these are forms of **E-**

Girl, WHAT you gonna DO with your MONEY?
Money Matters for Teens

COMMERCE. If you're already doing these things, stop doing them for free! Do your research to find out how to make money off of them and then legally form your business. Talk to the trusted adults in your life for guidance on the best way to do this.

No matter what option you choose, which doesn't have to necessarily be one of the above, I want you to keep your options open. I want you to dream the *unthinkable*. Don't ever think that because you are young that you are limited! **YOU** can **DO** whatever you put your heart to! Period! Don't allow yourself or anyone else to tell you that you cannot do something.

Now go **DO** it, but make sure you do your research first so you can do it RIGHT!

Discuss with an adult what Financial Freedom options you desire. Record the results:

_____

_____

_____

_____

_____

_____

_____

Girl, WHAT you gonna DO with your MONEY?
Money Matters for Teens

Lesson:

1. How can I be free to be me as a teen?

   _____
   _____
   _____

2. Write down various types of Investments:

   _____
   _____
   _____

3. Write down other types of Investments (from your research) that were not listed above:

   _____
   _____
   _____

   Which ones do YOU like?

   _____
   _____
   _____

4. Get to know a grown up that may be doing some of the things above and ask if you can interview and/or shadow them.

Girl, WHAT you gonna DO with your MONEY?
Money Matters for Teens

Key Words for Financial Freedom

Here are a few vocabulary words I want you to research and discuss with an adult.

Write the definitions below:

e-Commerce _____
_____
_____

Investor _____
_____
_____

Landlord _____
_____
_____

Intellectual Properties _____
_____
_____

Commodities _____
_____
_____

Girl, WHAT you gonna DO with your MONEY?
Money Matters for Teens

Key Words for Financial Freedom (continued)

Business _____

_____

_____

Partnership _____

_____

_____

Patents _____

_____

_____

Royalties _____

_____

_____

5
Failures
(Reflecting on your WHY)

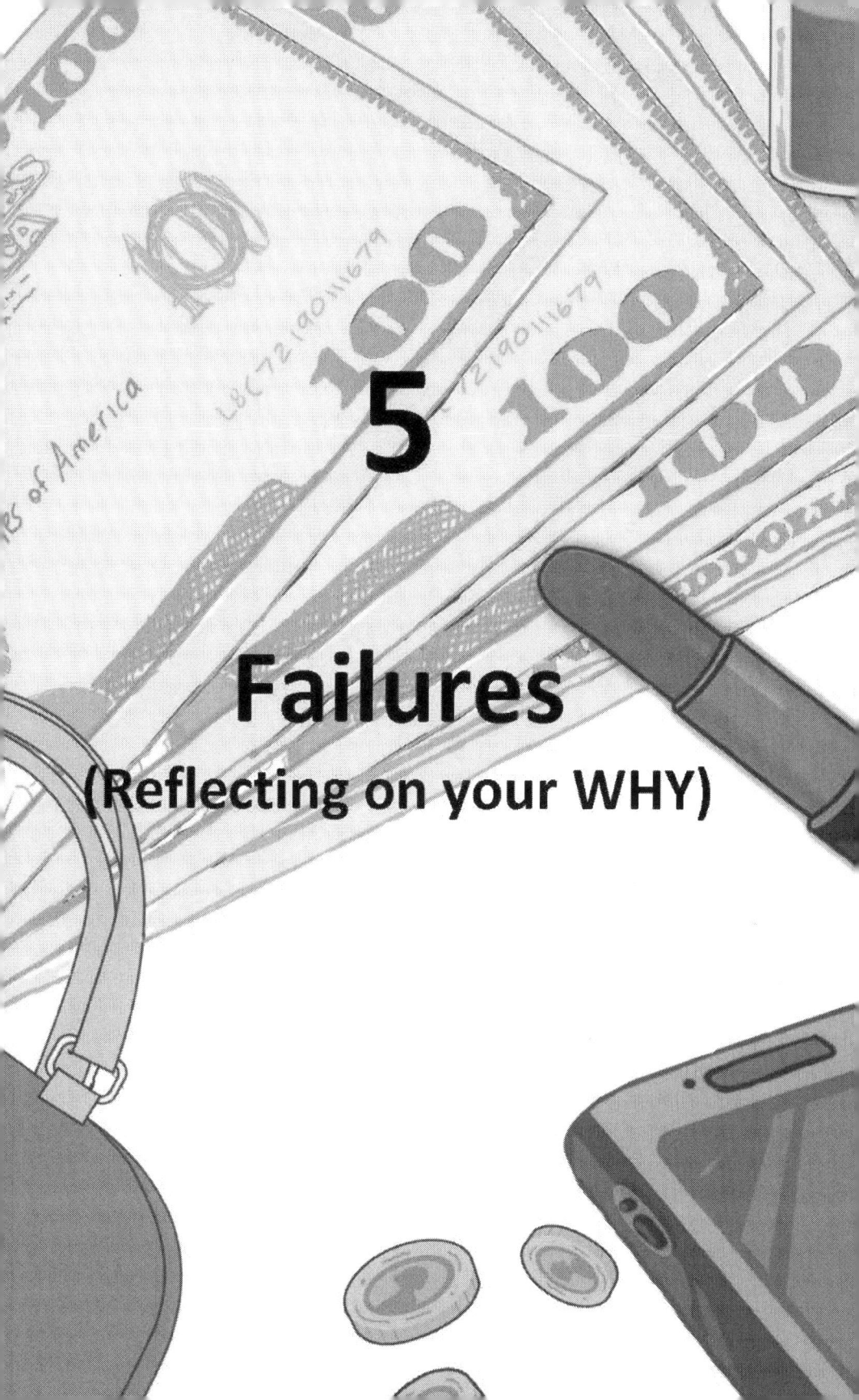

Girl, WHAT you gonna DO with your MONEY?
Money Matters for Teens

Girl, WHAT you gonna DO with your MONEY?
Money Matters for Teens

FAILURES

Like most, I've failed at staying focused on a goal and saving money. But the small voice on the inside of me never allowed me to quit. I never had the desire to simply give up.

My story is simple: I was raised one way but I had a dream to succeed. I saw myself being successful and that's what I chose to believe. I educated myself and did something about my situation. Yes, I had moments that I started and stopped but I never gave up and I don't want you to give up either.

You may find along the way that you start to save or be responsible with your money and then something happens and you lose track. DON'T give up! Don't let one set-back cause you to see yourself as a failure.

Think about WHY you are being responsible with your money in the first place. Always go back to your WHY. Know that no matter what your situation is now, you have the power to write your own STORY. You have an amazing future ahead of you!

✍ What is your WHY? ✍

_____

_____

_____

_____

_____

Girl, WHAT you gonna DO with your MONEY?
Money Matters for Teens

✍ What is YOUR story? ✍

Girl, WHAT you gonna DO with your MONEY?
Money Matters for Teens

✍ What is YOUR story (continued)? ✍

Girl, WHAT you gonna DO with your MONEY?
Money Matters for Teens

6
See Believe DO

Girl, WHAT you gonna DO with your MONEY?
Money Matters for Teens

Girl, WHAT you gonna DO with your MONEY?
Money Matters for Teens

SEE – BELIEVE – DO

There is no magic formula and there is nothing that makes me more special than you. YOU are quite special in your own way, so STRUT in *your* SPECIAL!

I want you to know that accomplishing your success is as simple as allowing yourself to dream (see); believing in yourself (believe) and taking action (do). Adding a combination of self-discipline and *delayed gratification* (which we discussed before), brought me to the place where I am today. A place where I work because I love to do what I do, not because I *have* to!

REMEMBER: If you do what you LOVE to do, you will never have to work hard. Although you must work your dream, it won't *feel* like hard work because it is what you LOVE to do. Believe me, there is a difference.

I want you to search your heart and think of what makes *you* happy. Think about what comes natural to you and what you would do even if you never got paid for it. Think about the things your friends or others may say are difficult for them to do but are easy for you. I want you to note that what comes easy for you, may very well be the one thing that helps *you* be financially free one day. Could you imagine that? Could you dare to imagine that you could actually make money from doing what you LOVE?

The more you see yourself doing what you love to do, the more you will believe in yourself. But remember, all the seeing and believing in the world will not bring forth any of your dreams. You also must DO something about it. So let's GO! Go **DO** it!

Do the following exercises:

Girl, WHAT you gonna DO with your MONEY?
Money Matters for Teens

SEE

Write down how you **SEE** yourself financially in the future:

_____

_____

_____

_____

BELIEVE

Write down *your* **BELIEFS** about how your financial life will be:

_____

_____

_____

_____

DO

Write down what you're going to **DO** about your financial life:

_____

_____

_____

Girl, WHAT you gonna DO with your MONEY?

7
Educate Yourself

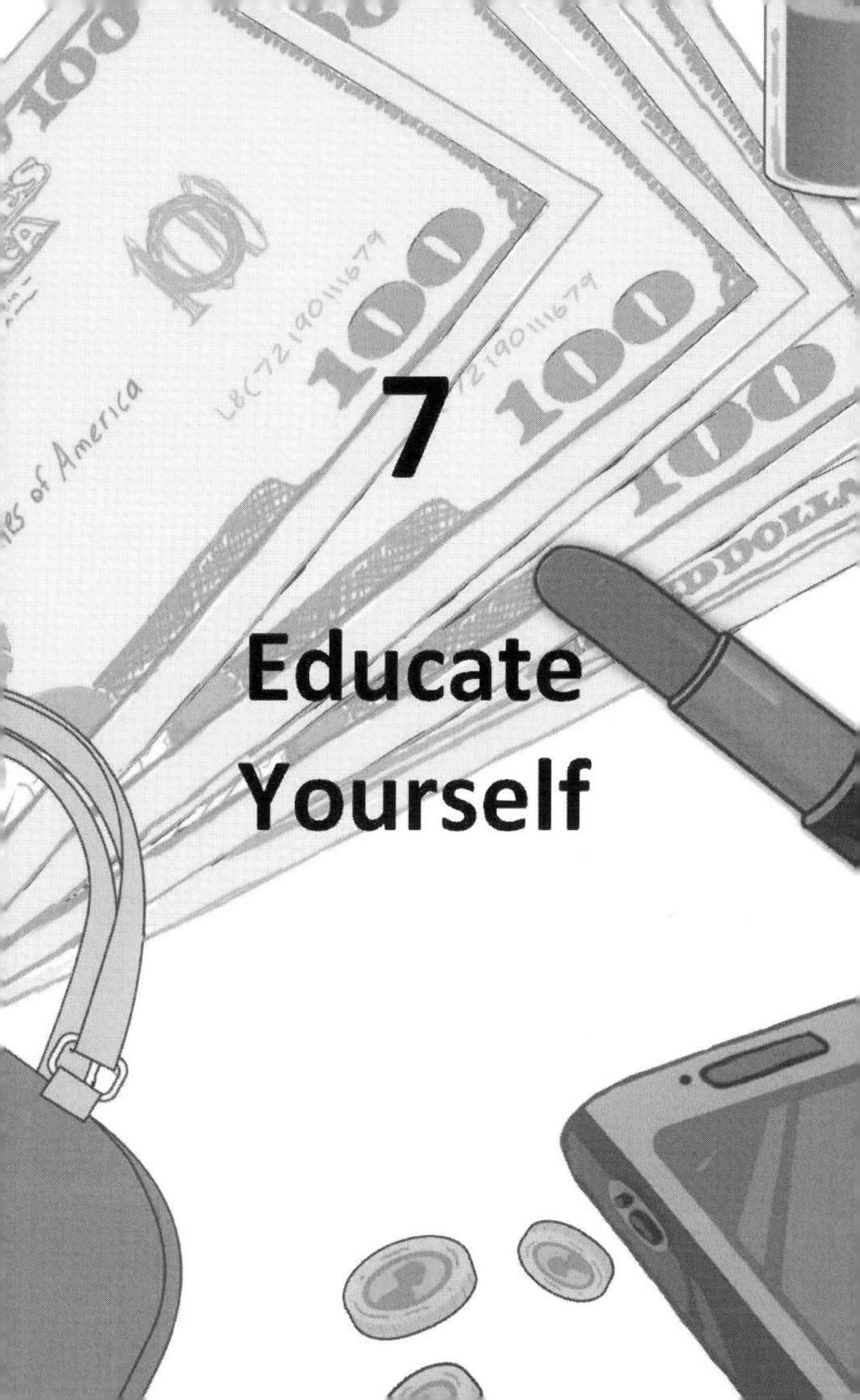

Girl, WHAT you gonna DO with your MONEY?
Money Matters for Teens

Girl, WHAT you gonna DO with your MONEY?
Money Matters for Teens

EDUCATE YOURSELF! YES, YOU CAN!

You can have Financial Freedom at a young age! Some of you will grasp this concept early, however, the idea may be a little more challenging for others.

Most of us are not taught these principles at a young age, if at all. And we may not get these principles in school either. I want to challenge you to use this book as a guide to help you dig deeper and study more.

Start studying words like loans, mortgages, stocks, bonds, real estate investing, intellectual properties, commodities and ask grownups questions. **Ask LOTS of questions!** Have multiple conversations with your parents or any adult figure that you trust. It may be uncomfortable at first, but you can do it!

Ask questions like:

What are investments?

How do I get credit?

Do you save money, Mom and Dad?

Again, these may be tough questions, but I assure you that adults are more than willing to answer, especially the ones who want you to be successful. You may even get closer to the family members that you ask or make new friends with strangers. I mean, WHO doesn't like the thought of having enough money to survive?

Make it happen! **YOU can DO it!**

Girl, WHAT you gonna DO with your MONEY?
Money Matters for Teens

Financial Education Homework

Answer the following questions to guide you as you are financially educating yourself:

1. Where can you find free information about money?

   _____

   _____

   _____

2. Ask an adult you trust to take you to the bank with him/her. Ask him/her to explain checking, savings and other money questions you may have. *If you're old enough, consider opening your own bank account.*

   Write his/her answer below:

   _____

   _____

   _____

3. Meet the banker while you're at the bank. Get their business card for future reference.

4. Write the name and address of the bank for future reference:

   _____

   _____

   _____

8

What Do I Do Now?

(Taking financial responsibility)

Girl, WHAT you gonna DO with your MONEY?
Money Matters for Teens

Girl, WHAT you gonna DO with your MONEY?
Money Matters for Teens

WHAT DO I DO NOW?
TAKING FINANCIAL RESPONSIBILITY!

The path to financial freedom is YOURS! Remember, YOU must **see**, **believe** *and* **DO** something in order to take charge of your financial life.

On the path to financial freedom you must first define what it means to you as an individual (discovering your "why"). Take time to explore the path that leads to how you really feel about money (what you believe).

REMEMBER: It's never too soon to block out the noise and explore your own beliefs.

> See, Believe & DO in order to take charge of your financial life.

You may ask, *So WHAT can I do NOW about money at THIS age?* I am so glad you asked!

Let's focus on a few simple steps by recapping the previous pages of this book.

1. Take time to LEARN about money.
2. Explore ideas of how *you* can make money.
3. Ask A LOT of questions!
4. REPEAT

Girl, WHAT you gonna DO with your MONEY?
Money Matters for Teens

And, again, remember to **See** yourself financially free, **Believe** you can and **Do** something about it!

YES, you can; it doesn't matter your age!

Brainstorm and write any questions you may still have:

_____

_____

_____

_____

_____

_____

_____

Girl! WHAT you gonna DO with your MONEY?

Girl, WHAT you gonna DO with your MONEY?
Money Matters for Teens

What about TODAY?

TODAY I STILL dream and I want YOU to dream too!

It is my hope that this book helps to educate, stimulate and motivate you. I hope this book provokes questions and pushes you to your financial destiny! If you learn nothing else from this book, I want to impress upon you that regardless of the success and pleasures that I enjoy, I am an *everyday* person, living my *everyday* life. I also want you to know that you are just as special as I am!

If I can do it, so can YOU!

Peace & Blessings,

Ti'Juana A. Gholson, MA

    Owner and Founder of TAG Consulting, LLC &
  L.I.P.S. ™ (Ladies Impacting Professional Systems)

Girl, WHAT you gonna DO with your MONEY?
Money Matters for Teens

ABOUT THE AUTHOR

Ti'Juana A. Gholson, Speaker/Author/Coach and member of The Maximized Life Coaching and Mentoring Team, is a Demonstrational Life & Business Coach specializing in program development, strategic and financial planning as well as business structuring. As a serial entrepreneur, Ti'Juana provides EVERYDAY mentorship and coaching to small business owners and contract professionals through her company TAG Consulting LLC.

She is also the founder of a business network called L.I.P.S.TM, (Ladies Impacting Professional Systems), where she meets with a group of women business owners twice a month to discuss business related concerns as they mastermind new business ideas and ventures. Ti'Juana enjoys spending time with youth groups and teaching youth about money. She believes it's never too early to learn about *money matters!*

Ti'Juana lives by the motto "Maximize YOUR Life" and she strives to **live her life on purpose with NO apologies and NO regrets**!

Girl, WHAT you gonna DO with your MONEY?
Money Matters for Teens

LET'S CONNECT!

Let's Connect

Get your FREE 10-minute phone coaching session with Ti'Juana at:

www.tijuanagholson.com

For more tips and to connect with other readers of this book.

Join our Facebook Community Page

@Ti'Juana Gholson the Author

Girl, WHAT you gonna DO with your MONEY?
Money Matters for Teens

Girl, WHAT you gonna DO with your MONEY?
Money Matters for Teens

FINANCE JOURNAL

Use this section of the book to write your financial story. When ideas come to mind, write them down. This journal will be a tool and a resource to keep you accountable and help you accomplish your goals!

Take time to see yourself being where you want to be financially one day. Dare to DREAM! Don't think ANY idea is too big to accomplish. YOU are amazing and **YOU** can **DO** it!

Girl! WHAT you gonna DO with your MONEY!

Girl, WHAT you gonna DO with your MONEY?
Money Matters for Teens

Today's Date: _____

Girl, WHAT you gonna DO with your MONEY?
Money Matters for Teens

Today's Date: _____

Girl, WHAT you gonna DO with your MONEY?
Money Matters for Teens

Today's Date: _____

Girl, WHAT you gonna DO with your MONEY?
Money Matters for Teens

Today's Date: _____

Girl, WHAT you gonna DO with your MONEY?
Money Matters for Teens

Today's Date: _____

Girl, WHAT you gonna DO with your MONEY?
Money Matters for Teens

Today's Date: _____

_____
_____
_____
_____
_____
_____
_____
_____
_____
_____
_____
_____
_____
_____
_____
_____
_____
_____

Girl, WHAT you gonna DO with your MONEY?
Money Matters for Teens

Today's Date: _____

Girl, WHAT you gonna DO with your MONEY?
Money Matters for Teens

Today's Date: _____

Girl, WHAT you gonna DO with your MONEY?
Money Matters for Teens

Today's Date: _____

_____
_____
_____
_____
_____
_____
_____
_____
_____
_____
_____
_____
_____
_____
_____
_____
_____

Girl, WHAT you gonna DO with your MONEY?
Money Matters for Teens

Today's Date: _____

Girl, WHAT you gonna DO with your MONEY?
Money Matters for Teens

Today's Date: _____

_____
_____
_____
_____
_____
_____
_____
_____
_____
_____
_____
_____
_____
_____
_____
_____
_____
_____
_____
_____

Girl, WHAT you gonna DO with your MONEY?
Money Matters for Teens

Today's Date: _____

Girl, WHAT you gonna DO with your MONEY?
Money Matters for Teens

Today's Date: _____

Girl, WHAT you gonna DO with your MONEY?
Money Matters for Teens

Today's Date: _____

Girl, WHAT you gonna DO with your MONEY?
Money Matters for Teens

Today's Date: _____

Girl, WHAT you gonna DO with your MONEY?
Money Matters for Teens

Today's Date: _____

Girl, WHAT you gonna DO with your MONEY?
Money Matters for Teens

Today's Date: _____

Girl, WHAT you gonna DO with your MONEY?
Money Matters for Teens

Today's Date: _____

Girl, WHAT you gonna DO with your MONEY?
Money Matters for Teens

Today's Date: _____

_____
_____
_____
_____
_____
_____
_____
_____
_____
_____
_____
_____
_____
_____
_____
_____
_____
_____
_____
_____
_____
_____

Girl, WHAT you gonna DO with your MONEY?
Money Matters for Teens

Today's Date: _____

Girl, WHAT you gonna DO with your MONEY?
Money Matters for Teens

Today's Date: _____

Girl, WHAT you gonna DO with your MONEY?
Money Matters for Teens

Today's Date: _____

Girl, WHAT you gonna DO with your MONEY?
Money Matters for Teens

Today's Date: _____

_____
_____
_____
_____
_____
_____
_____
_____
_____
_____
_____
_____
_____
_____
_____
_____
_____
_____
_____
_____

Girl, WHAT you gonna DO with your MONEY?
Money Matters for Teens

Today's Date: _____

Made in the USA
Middletown, DE
20 April 2019